EMOTIONALLY IMMATURE PARENT:
healing from a distance and recovering from childhood rejection

Tyler Jones

Table of content

Chapter 1

Emotional immature parent

Genuinely energetic (EI) gatekeepers are both bewildering and devastating. It's challenging to treasure a discouraged parent who expects honor and extraordinary treatment yet endeavors to at the same time control and excuse you.

A relationship with an EI parent is portrayed by not getting your sentiments met. They are scarcely the slightest bit about experiencing significant closeness in which two people come to know and see each other at a significant level. This normal sharing of most significant opinions makes a phenomenal, significant bond that makes the individuals important to each other, but this isn't something EI gatekeepers feel content with doing.

Every so often you glimpse a passing hankering in them for certifiable affiliation, and this keeps you associating with them. Unfortunately, the more you associate, the further they die down, cautious about certifiable closeness. Like being in a stirred up around town floor with someone is moving away from you in ideal synchrony to your undertakings to move close. Their solicitations for thought joined with watchfulness about closeness, make a push-me, pull-me relationship that leaves you unsatisfied and genuinely barren. You care about your people, but you can't gravitate toward the eventual result of having a certifiable relationship.

At the point when you handle them, nevertheless, your experiences will sound great to you — in this manner will your up close and personal discouragement. By comprehending the EI mind, you will need to deal with your EI gatekeepers — or any earnestly adolescent individual (EIP) — in habits that free you from their significant impulses and make a more guaranteed relationship considering understanding what you can and can't expect from them

Growing up with EI parents fosters emotional loneliness. Although your parents may have been physically present, emotionally you may have felt left on your own. Although you may feel a family bond with your EI parent, that's very different from an emotionally secure parent-child relationship. EI parents like to tell their children what to do, but they are uncomfortable with emotional nurturing. EI parents may take good care of you when you're sick, but they don't know what to do with hurt feelings or broken hearts. As a result, they may seem artificial and awkward when trying to soothe a distressed child.

EI parents' self-absorption and limited empathy make interactions with them feel one-sided. It's as if they're imprisoned in their self-involvement. When you try to share something important to you, they're likely to talk over you, change the subject, start talking about themselves, or dismiss what you're saying.

Children of EI parents often know a great deal more about their parents' issues than the parents know about theirs. Although EI parents require your attention when they're upset, they rarely offer listening or empathy when you're distressed. Instead of sitting with you and letting you get it all out, EI parents typically offer superficial solutions, tell you not to worry, or even get irritated with you for being upset. Their heart feels closed like there's no place you can go inside them for compassion or comfort.

You feel coerced and trapped
EI parents insist you put them first and let them run the show. To this end, they coerce you with shame, guilt, or fear until you do what they want. They can flare into blame and anger if you don't toe the line. Many people use the word manipulation for these kinds of emotional coercions, but I think that word is misleading. These behaviors are more like survival instincts.

They do whatever's necessary to feel more in control and protected at the moment, oblivious to what it might cost you. You can also feel trapped by their superficial style of relating. Because EI parents relate in a superficial, egocentric way, talking with them is often boring.

They stick to conversation topics they feel safe with, which quickly become stagnant and repetitious.

EI parents are extremely self-referential, meaning that everything is always about them. They expect you to accept second place when it comes to their needs. They elevate their interests to the point that yours feel downgraded. They're not looking for an equal relationship. They want blind allegiance to their need to be considered first. Without a parent willing to give your emotional needs a high priority, it can leave you feeling insecure. Wondering if a parent will think of you or have your back can make you vulnerable to stress, anxiety, and depression. These are reasonable reactions to a childhood environment in which you couldn't trust a parent to notice your needs or protect you from things that overwhelmed you.

They won't be emotionally intimate or vulnerable with you

Although they're highly reactive emotionally, EI parents avoid their deeper feelings (McCullough et al. 2003). They fear being emotionally exposed and often hide behind a defensive exterior. They even avoid tenderness toward their children because this might make them too vulnerable. They also worry that showing love might undermine their power as parents because power is all they think they've got.

Even though EI parents hide their vulnerable feelings, they can show plenty of intense emotion when they fight with their partner, complain about their problems, blow off steam, or fly into a fury with their kids. When upset, they don't look like they are at all afraid of what they feel.

However, these one-sided eruptions of emotion are merely releases of emotional pressures. That's not the same thing as a willingness to be open to real emotional connection. For this reason, comforting them is hard to do. They want you to feel how upset they are, but they resist the intimacy of real comfort. If you try to make them feel better, they may stiff-arm you away. This poor receptive capacity (McCullough 1997) prevents them from taking in any comfort and connection you try to offer.

They communicate through emotional contagion
Instead of talking about their feelings, EI people express themselves nonverbally through emotional contagion

Like small children, EI parents want you to intuit what they feel without them saying anything. They feel hurt and angry when you don't guess their needs, expecting you to know what they want. If you protest that they didn't tell you what they wanted, their reaction is, "If you loved me, you would've known." They expect you to stay constantly attuned to them. It's legitimate for a baby or small child to expect such attention from their parents, but not for a parent to expect that from their child.

 They don't respect your boundaries or individuality
EI parents don't understand the point of boundaries. They think boundaries imply rejection, meaning you don't care enough about them to give them free access to your life. This is why they act incredulous, offended, or hurt if you ask them to respect your privacy. They feel loved only when you let them interrupt you at any time. EI parents seek dominant and privileged roles in which they don't have to respect others' boundaries. EI parents also don't respect

your individuality because they don't see the need for it.

 Family and roles are sacrosanct to them, and they don't understand why you should want space or an individual identity apart from them. They don't understand why you can't just be like them, think like them, and have the same beliefs and values. You are their child and, therefore, belong to them. Even when you're grown, they expect you to remain their compliant child or—if you insist on your own life—at least always follow their advice.

You do the emotional work in the relationship
Emotional work (Fraad, 2008) is the effort you make to emotionally adapt to other people's needs. Emotional work can be easy—such as being polite and pleasant—or deeply complicated, such as

trying hard to say the right thing to your distraught teenager.

Emotional work consists of empathy, common sense, awareness of motives, and anticipating how someone is likely to respond to your actions. When things go wrong in a relationship, the need for emotional work skyrockets. Apologizing, seeking reconciliation, and making amends are among the strenuous emotional labors that sustain healthy long-term relationships. But because EI parents lack interest in relationship repairs, reconnection efforts may fall to you. Instead of amends or apologies, EI parents often make things worse by projecting blame, accusing others, and disowning responsibility for their behavior. In a situation where it would seem easier just to go ahead and apologize, EI parents can be adamant that it was something you did—or failed to do—that warranted their hurtful behavior. If only you had known better and done what they asked, this problem never would've occurred.

 You lose your emotional autonomy and mental freedom
Because EI parents see you as an extension of themselves, they disregard your inner world of thoughts and feelings. Instead, they claim the sole right to judge your feelings as either sensible or unwarranted. They don't respect your emotional autonomy, your freedom, and your right to have your feelings. Because your thoughts should reflect theirs, they react with shock and disapproval if you have ideas that offend them. You are not free to consider certain things even in the privacy of your mind. ("Don't even think about it!") Your thoughts and feelings are filtered through their comfort level as either good or bad.
 They can be killjoys and even sadistic.

EI parents can be awful killjoys, both to their children and to other people. They rarely resonate with others' feelings, so they don't take pleasure in other people's happiness. Instead of enjoying their child's accomplishments, EI parents can react in ways that take the shine off the child's pride. They also are famous for deflating their children's dreams by reminding them about the depressing realities of adult life. the relationship.

Chapter 2

How emotionally immature parent affect their Children

Children start developing their emotions during the infancy stage, which lasts approximately from birth to the age of two years. During this stage, a great deal of initial learning occurs for the child, about their general environment and the people that are in it.
Much of this learning occurs through interactions with parents and observations of parental relations, who are the first and most prominent figures in a child's early life. Happiness, distress, and disgust are amongst the initial emotions to appear in children just a few months after birth. Later on, social emotions appear followed by the emotion of fear between the ages of two and four years. Generally, emotions start to differ as a child begins to mature.

So far, it is known that parents significantly influence the emotional development of their children. Parents do far more than meet the basic survival needs of their children, and research is increasingly finding that they have an enormous influence on a wide variety of health outcomes for their children, including behavioral habits, physical and mental health outcomes, and emotional development. In the past couple of decades, incredible effort and research have gone into understanding how inter-parental conflict might affect a child's ability to grow, develop and function healthily. For instance, nearly two-thirds of all studies included in one author's meta-analysis that related to the inter-parental conflict were published in the 1990s, demonstrating just how much interest has grown in recent years in this field.

In this regard, it is important to fill the gap in knowledge regarding what kinds of parental behaviors influence the emotional development of their children, and in what ways. It is important to explore how positive and negative parental behaviors influence the emotional development of children.

A research paper will conduct a meta-analysis of existing literature to answer the important question "does inter-parental conflict negatively affect the emotional security of children who are part of the family"?

the interparental conflict appears to be high globally and increasing. For instance, in Australia, researchers have found that inter-parental conflict affects millions of children annually. The number of reported family violence cases in Australia has increased in the last six years. Statistics indicate that nearly 25 percent of women experience abuse that is perpetuated by a partner at some point in their lives, and that this affects a minimum of one million children yearly. These statistics likely represent a gross underestimation, given that family conflict statistics are obtained from the police, child welfare, and family court data, which only captures the most severe forms of psychological, physical, and emotional abuse. Researchers have concluded that community prevalence of inter-parental conflict is likely much higher than these statistics indicate.

Increasingly there has also been far more international recognition of the enormous health burdens and economic consequences that both high and low-lying levels of inter-parental conflict can create. For instance, women who are regularly exposed to violence within their families are identified as being at a higher risk of experiencing significant and long-term negative mental and physical health outcomes. Research also indicates that reports of domestic violence tend to occur for parents that are younger, less educated, come from single or divorced families, and have higher levels of stress and alcohol-related problems. For children, the health effects associated with inter-parental conflict are numerous and include (but are not limited to) increased prevalence of mental health problems such as mood and anxiety disorders, attention deficit hyperactivity disorder, conduct or oppositional defiant disorder, as well as several physical health problems such as obesity, asthma, and accidental injury.

While most of the existing literature has focused on the most severe cases of domestic abuse-which might include physical, emotional, and sexual abuse-researchers are increasingly linking lower levels of inter-parental conflict to difficult child development. Thus, researchers are now recognizing that inter-parental conflict can include less severe but far more common types of conflict, including verbal conflict (such as disagreements, anger, hostility, or arguments) and lower levels of physical conflict (such as pushing, kicking, hitting or shoving). As such, findings in this field are increasingly becoming more generalizable to the rest of the population

Researchers and clinicians have long presumed that there is an important relationship between the quality of parental relationships and the emotional, physical, cognitive, and psychological development of their children. The link between inter-parental conflict and children's behavioral and emotional development dysfunction has been well-established for both intact and divorced families, Meta-analysis has found that the average effect size for inter-parental conflict on child development was between a small and medium effect which is near twice the effect size for the association between child adjustment and divorce. The inter-parental conflict is highest for households with children who are under the age of five years. Inter-parental and parent-child conflicts have been found to negatively impact children across all ages in terms of emotional, social, academic, and health problems, and children's risk becomes particularly high when parents are involved in a highly distressed marriage.

Children who experience significant conflict within their family will often have trouble with their social and emotional development and well-being. This is true for children who regularly hear their parents fighting-a phenomenon that has been referred to as 'background noise' in a child's upbringing, Even though the anger and conflict are not being directed right at the child, children can easily develop problems with their emotional security and regulation as a result. This often occurs because, from the earliest ages, children emulate what they see, often copying the behavior of their parents with other social relations. If children are used to witnessing conflict and poor emotional regulation regularly, this will be their understanding of social relationships as their social network expands later in life.

While the link between children's behavioral and emotional development and inter-parental conflict is accepted by researchers, there are often variations given that not all children who witness inter-parental conflict develop behavioral problems. For instance, marital dissatisfaction is a very broad construct, making it critical that researchers identify exactly what factors related to discordant marriages that are leading to the negative development outcomes of children.

As such, more recent research has sought to identify the characteristics of children who are exposed to interparental conflict, as well as their coping responses and contextual factors of the inter-parental conflict that may be affecting their adjustment problems findings suggest that rather than being the conflict itself that is leading to problems, there are more proximal processes that account for the relation between inter-parental conflict and the emergence of child behavioral problems.

Researchers like Rhoades have found that when studying the effects of inter-parental conflict on children's emotional development, it is more useful to consider children's responses to conflict as one potential proximal variable. These responses effectively indicate how children process and create meaning from the inter-parental conflict they witness, particularly concerning their own goals, desires, and needs. According to Rhoades, children's responses to conflict are important because:

Chapter 3

How children react to emotional immature parent

Their energy makes them clashing and genuinely conflicting, and they're thoughtless with respect to their young people's prerequisites once their own course of action turns out to be conceivably the chief part.

Legends and dreams have been depicting such monitors for quite a while. Consider how much dreams solidify abandoned young people who ought to find help from animals and various partners considering how their family are thoughtless, flabbergasted, or missing. In unambiguous records, the parent character is truly poisonous and the young people ought to take command of their determination. These records have been exceptional for quite a while since they correspond to a typical concordance: how young people ought to battle for themselves after their family have exculpated or abandoned them.

Obviously, youthful grown-up gatekeepers have been an issue since extra. Additionally, this subject of basic thoughtlessness by self-diverted gatekeepers can anyway be tracked down in the most persuasive records with respect to our standard society. In books, movies, and TV, the story of really overwhelming gatekeepers and the effects they have on their young people's lives makes for a rich subject. In unambiguous records, this parent-young person dynamic is the essential fixation; in others, it might be depicted all through the whole presence of an individual.

Having a lot of experience with contrasts in exceptionally close improvement gives you a technique for overseeing understanding the motivation driving why you can feel so genuinely disregarded paying little heed to what others' instances of friendship and connection. By embracing the opportunity of tremendous pre-adulthood, you can uphold more sensible hypotheses for other people, continuing on through the level of relationship possible with them as opposed to feeling hurt by their deficiency of response.

Among psychotherapists, it's for a critical period of time been seen that genuinely disengaging from heartbreaking gatekeepers is the technique for restoring concordance and opportunity. In any case, how could one do this? We do it by understanding what we are making due.

Precisely when you esteem their characteristics, you'll have the choice to choose for yourself what level of relationship might be possible, or incomprehensible, with your family. Understanding this licenses us to return to ourselves, happening with life from our own further nature rather than focusing on gatekeepers who won't change. Understanding their exceptionally close pre-adulthood frees us from basic weakness as we value their inconsiderateness wasn't about us, but about them. Unequivocally when we see the protection for why they can't be extraordinary, we can finally be freed from our slip-up with them, as well as our solicitations concerning our own brightness

Chapter 4

How to handle emotionally immature parent

Self-involved, and they give mixed messages to their children growing up about their lovability and individuality. Parents' emotional immaturity denies a child the deep sense of being felt and seen, which hinders a child's budding self-identity.

Adult children of emotionally immature parents are often left feeling like they can't make it on their own or somehow that they're not enough. These same parents are often self-involved, and they give mixed messages to their children growing up about their lovability and individuality. Parents' emotional immaturity denies a child the deep sense of being felt and seen, which hinders a child's budding self-identity.

The adult child having a conversation with his father
Emotionally immature parents rarely extend empathy or provide emotional support to their children because their parents' needs and insecurities compete with their child's emotional needs.

A parent who lacks emotional intelligence will continue to eclipse the adult child's emotional legitimacy. The mixed and unclear signals can be crazy-making, causing self-doubt and a longing to be heard.

Adult children often continue to try to get their needs met through other people who cannot understand another's experience. Since feeling heard is a core human need, it can be excruciating to be raised by an infantile parent. If you are reading this blog, maybe you're trying to make sense of what you feel and gain some understanding.

self-soothe, or self-regulate. Emotionally immature parents neglect to provide secure attachment for their children.
 Once you are taught to doubt yourself, you start looking to others for direction, trusting other people's perspectives over your own. Instead of knowing what you think and feel, you become preoccupied with just being accepted."

 Passive parents who are unengaged in their child's life and often too overwhelmed to interact with the child maturely.
 Driven parents who are always busy, busy, busy either working or simply preoccupied with self-centeredness,

making it near impossible to truly connect on any meaningful level.

Emotional parents who are self-involved often neglect their children. Their infantile nature keeps them centered on themselves with no bandwidth for caring for their children.

Rejecting parents who are emotionally unavailable and detach completely. These parents don't acknowledge their child's efforts for attention (or just enough to keep the child craving more) or openly criticize and reject their child.

Now, of course, just like any categorization or labeling, there are overlapping and common denominators in each group. A very loving parent can have some of these symptoms since they are human, but these parents show up lovingly more often and provide secure attachment rather than parents with insecure attachment styles. With the emotionally immature, inadequacies occupy their full attention and make them ill-equipped to provide secure attachment for their children.

The good news is that your childhood need not define you. You can build emotional fitness and learn to be emotionally savvy. Learning some critical emotional intelligence skills will provide you with a solid foundation for supporting yourself, give you tools to sort through conflicting emotions, heal your pain, and live more confidently in life. Emotional intelligence offers a way through the pain of feeling unheard, unseen, and invisible and lights the way to wholeness.

An emotionally immature parent tells a young man how to feel

Chapter 5

Consequences of Growing Up with Emotionally Immature Parents

Exactly when you have lived with an adolescent, difficult to reach, or very self-important parent, you could regardless feel shocked, discouragement, unfairness, and surrender could stand by you.

You'll need to encourage an up close and personal turn of events and sensible pieces of information into your impressions of shock and hopelessness to retouch. Exactly when your sentiments aren't met, track down approaches to being more present with your opinions and sentiments. Think about authentic information in your exacerbation. Remain related to yourself without wandering off into fantasy land or dulling yourself.

Chapter 6

Patterns that are possibly developed when growing up

With neglectful parents, you may neglect your own emotions or self-care.

 With a driven parent who doesn't make time for their children, you may seek to prove yourself worthy of love through an obsession with work or over-giving to others.

With immature, unavailable, or selfish parents, you may be inaccessible to your friends, partner, or children. Or you may protect yourself with defenses; being vulnerable and open can feel too threatening.

With a reactive or emotional parent, you might avoid conflict and stuff your needs or emotions, caretaking to the people in your life.

With a rejecting parent, you may reject yourself and deny your own needs to keep others happy.

With difficult or autocratic parents where there is little consideration for your perspective or feelings, you may not be in touch with your needs or feel paralyzed when making decisions because you never got practice growing up.

However, no matter what kind of childhood you experienced, you can connect with the compass of your true self, learning the genuine nature of relationships beginning with yourself.

The First Step to Emotional Maturity Is Self-Compassion

One of the first steps of healing and building resiliency as an adult after a painful childhood is compassionately loving yourself. You must have self-compassion and be present to yourself when emotionally immature parents are unable to be there for you. Whether your parent's behavior is self-involved or rejecting, whether they're passive or driven and ignore you and your needs, start by healing yourself through self-compassion.

What does it mean to have self-compassion? It means being kind to yourself when you are struggling or having a hard time. It means accepting that you may feel helpless or lonely at times when your parents are unable to give you what you need. Being present to your own emotions and pain when your parents are clueless about how to be present to you and your experience is having compassion for your experience.

Being kind to yourself will help buffer the hard truth that you cannot change them, only yourself and your response.

Chapter 7

How to Lovingly and Firmly Deal with Emotionally Immature Parents

"I can see that my decision has disappointed you. Additionally, it's indispensable to me to settle on the ideal choice for me."
"Do you have any considerations on how we can endeavor to make more correspondence and balance?"

These thoughtful responses show understanding of their opinions and the situation. Sympathy prepares for a more significant sharing of opinions and manufactures an ordinarily satisfying relationship. This sort of correspondence enables the two players to share their perspectives and needs without epic confrontations or sets feeling horrendous.

Balance self-compassion and sympathy for your people by articulating your contemplations without getting protected. This directly shows improvement and respect. Exactly when we distinguish, in like manner consider all the more obvious trade about what our exercises mean for each other in associations.

The posterity of earnest adolescent gatekeepers needs to sort out some way to find love in themselves and give self-compassion considering the way that their people now and again can't maintain them in an accomplished, appreciating way.

Give compassion and love to yourself, and you'll be significantly more inclined to have further developed results with your people. Genuine pieces of information lead to care and begin to lay out a fresher and all the more certain point of convergence for your experiences.